P9-ELG-200

BIOGRAPHY

by Natalie M. Rosinsky

CONTRA COSTA COUNTY LIBRARY

3 1901 04400 7773

Compass Point Books ✦ Minneapolis, Minnesota

Compass Point Books
3109 West 50th Street, #115
Minneapolis, MN 55410

Copyright © 2008 by Compass Point Books
All rights reserved. No part of this book may be reproduced without written permission
from the publisher. The publisher takes no responsibility for the use of any of the
materials or methods described in this book, nor for the products thereof.
Printed in the United States of America.

 This book was manufactured with paper containing
at least 10 percent post-consumer waste.

Managing Editor: Catherine Neitge
Designer: ticktock Entertainment Ltd
Page Production: Bobbie Nuytten
Photo Researcher: Svetlana Zhurkin
Library Consultant: Kathleen Baxter

Art Director: Jaime Martens
Creative Director: Keith Griffin
Editorial Director: Nick Healy

Compass Point Books would like to acknowledge the contributions of Tish Farrell, who
authored earlier Write Your Own books and whose supporting text is reused in part herein.

Library of Congress Cataloging-in-Publication Data
Rosinsky, Natalie M. (Natalie Myra)
  Write your own biography / by Natalie M. Rosinsky.
      p. cm. — (Write your own)
  Includes bibliographical references and index.
  ISBN-13: 978-0-7565-3366-3 (library binding)
  ISBN-10: 0-7565-3366-X (library binding)
1. Biography as a literary form—Juvenile literature. 2. Biography as a literary
form—Study and teaching (Elementary) I. Title. II. Series.
  CT22.R67 2008
   808'.06692—dc22   2007011471

Visit Compass Point Books on the Internet at *www.compasspointbooks.com*
or e-mail your request to *custserv@compasspointbooks.com*

About the Author
Natalie M. Rosinsky is the award-winning author of
more than 100 works for young readers. She earned
graduate degrees from the University of Wisconsin-
Madison and has been a high school teacher and
college professor as well as a corporate trainer. Natalie,
who reads and writes in Mankato, Minnesota, says,
"My love of reading led me to write. I take pleasure in
framing ideas, crafting words, detailing other lives and
places. I am delighted to share these joys with young
authors in the Write Your Own series of books."

Get a Life

*What leads someone to become a real-life hero or villain? How different are famous scientists, artists, athletes, and politicians from you and people you know? How well **do** you know the people in your family and community? What events and decisions shaped **their** lives? As a writer of biographies, you will discover and reveal answers to these fascinating questions.*

As you journey through another's life, you may find the answers you seek in the distant past or faraway countries. Sometimes the answers may be as nearby as a family photo album. This book is a key that will help you unlock and explain the mysteries of someone else's life. It contains brainstorming and training activities to sharpen your writing skills. Tips and advice from famous writers and examples from their own work will also help you on this adventure of a lifetime.

CONTENTS

HOW TO USE THIS BOOK

WANT TO BE A WRITER?

This book is the perfect place to start. It aims to give you the tools to write your own biography. Learn how to craft believable portraits of people and tell their stories with satisfying beginnings, middles, and endings. Examples from famous books appear throughout, with tips and techniques from published authors to help you on your way.

Get the writing habit

Do timed and regular practice. Real writers learn to write even when they don't particularly feel like it.

Create a biography-writing zone.

Keep a journal.

Carry a notebook—record interesting events and note how people behave and speak.

Generate ideas

Find a person whose story you want to tell. What are his or her problems and accomplishments?

Brainstorm to find out everything about your chosen person.

Research settings, events, and other people in this person's life.

Create a timeline of your chosen person's life.

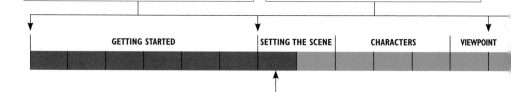

GETTING STARTED | SETTING THE SCENE | CHARACTERS | VIEWPOINT

You can follow your progress by using the bar located on the bottom of each page. The orange color tells you how far along the biography writing process you have gotten. As the blocks are filled out, your biography will be growing.

4

Plan

What is your biography about?

What happens?

Plan beginning, middle, and end.

Write a synopsis or create storyboards.

Write

Write the first draft, then put it aside for a while.

Check spelling and dialogue —does it flow?

Remove unnecessary words.

Does the biography have a good title and satisfying ending?

Avoid clichés.

Publish

Write or print the final draft.

Always keep a copy for yourself.

Send your biography to children's magazines, Internet writing sites, competitions, or school magazines.

SYNOPSES AND PLOTS	WINNING WORDS	SCINTILLATING SPEECH	HINTS AND TIPS	THE NEXT STEP

When you get to the end of the bar, your book is ready to go! You are an author! You now need to decide what to do with your book and what your next project should be. Perhaps it will be another biography, or maybe something completely different.

THE "WRITE" LIFESTYLE

Biographers may do research in the library, on the Internet, or in family records and albums. They sometimes travel short or long distances to interview people and see places connected to the life story they are writing.

Just like all writers, biographers need handy tools and a safe, comfortable place for their work. A computer can make writing quicker, but it is not essential.

What you need

These materials will help you organize your ideas and your findings:

- small notebook that you carry everywhere
- paper for writing activities
- pencils or pens with different colored ink
- large sheets of paper for drawing a timeline
- index cards for recording facts
- files or folders to keep your fact-finding organized and safe
- dictionary, thesaurus, and encyclopedia

Find your writing place

Think about where you as a writer feel most comfortable and creative. Author Ernest Hemingway did most of his writing standing up, while Mark Twain often wrote in bed! Perhaps a spot in your bedroom works best for you.

Possibly a corner in the public library is better. If your writing place is outside your home, store your writing materials in a take-along bag or backpack.

Create a biography-writing zone

- Play some of your favorite music or music that the person you are writing about might have liked.
- Use earplugs if you write best when it is quiet.
- Decorate your space with pictures of your subject or pictures of places or objects important to him or her.
- Place objects that hold good memories from your own life around your space.

CASE STUDY

Biographer Pam Munoz Ryan lives with four noisy children and two dogs. She turned a spare bedroom in her home into the quiet office space she needs for writing. She enjoys wearing comfortable slippers as she walks to her office and works there.

Follow the writer's golden rule

Once you have chosen your writing space, go there regularly and often. It is all right to do other kinds of writing there— such as a diary or letters—as long as you *keep on writing!*

Before you can write fascinating life stories, you have to build up your writing "muscles." Just as an athlete lifts weights or a musician practices scales, you must train regularly. You cannot wait until you are in the mood or feel especially inspired.

Tips and techniques

Set a regular amount of time and a schedule for your writing. It could be 10 minutes every morning before breakfast or one hour twice a week after supper. Then, come rain or shine, stick to your schedule.

Now it's your turn

Unlock your imagination

Begin your writing practice with some timed brainstorming. Go to your writing place. Close your eyes for a minute and relax. Think about what the word *hero* brings to mind. Now open your eyes and write down the phrases "A hero is" and "A hero does." For the next five minutes, complete these phrases with any words that pop into your head. Scribble away! Let the ideas pour out onto the paper the way water gushes out of a faucet or fountain. Now stop. You are on your way to being a writer of biographies.

Now it's your turn

Make the real-life connection

Look over your lists from the last exercise. Which people in your life, the news, or history have these qualities? Take five minutes to jot these names down. Now circle one of them. Add the words "is a hero because." For the next 10 minutes, finish this phrase with as many reasons as come to mind. If you wish, add how you feel about these heroic deeds. Do not stop, and do not worry about correct punctuation or writing in complete sentences. Let your ideas flow. You may have just found the subject of your biography.

Now that you have some hefty writing muscles, you are ready to tackle your new biography project.

CASE STUDY

Kathleen Krull got her idea for a biography of Olympic athlete Wilma Rudolph (far right) from reading the newspaper right after Rudolph's death. The runner's obituary mentioned that she had overcome polio. Krull did not know much about sports, but she had lived with a similar disease. She believed Rudolph's triumph over illness made the athlete an exceptionally heroic person.

A LIVELY APPROACH

For hundreds of years, people wrote biographies only of heroic or successful people. If there were unpleasant or shameful events in these famous people's lives, biographers omitted or downplayed such information. Today though, biographies of heroes usually include their flaws and failings. In the 20th and 21st centuries, biographies have even been written about people whose evil deeds made them notorious villains. Biographies are also written about ordinary people as well as famous ones. These books help readers understand what everyday life was like at particular times and places in the past. Before you choose someone as the subject of your biography, consider all these possibilities. Add life to your decision making here by reading some biographies, too.

CASE STUDY

African-American author Tonya Bolden was inspired to write the biography of an ordinary, rather than a famous, person—Maritcha Remond Lyons. *Maritcha: A Nineteenth-Century American Girl* has won awards for its portrait of a determined young African-American. Bolden says that Maritcha, born in 1848, was a native New Yorker as is she. Bolden admires Maritcha and considers her a personal role model.

CASE STUDY

Writer James Cross Giblin's biography of Charles Lindbergh (left) includes the poor decisions and bad judgment calls this pioneering aviator sometimes made. Giblin tellingly titled this award-winning book *Charles A. Lindbergh: A Human Hero*. The author has also written an award-winning biography of one of the 20th century's greatest villains, Nazi leader Adolf Hitler. Giblin's own childhood during World War II partly inspired him to write *The Life and Death of Adolf Hitler*. He remembers war news constantly blaring from radios when he was a boy.

FIND YOUR VOICE

Reading many books will help you discover your own style of writing—your writer's voice. Every good writer has a style of writing that is unique to that person. It takes lots of practice to acquire this unique voice. Writers continue to develop their voices throughout their lives.

Finding your writer's voice

Once you start reading as a writer, you will notice how writers have their own rhythm, style, and range of language that stay the same throughout a book. Jean Fritz (author of *Where Do You Think You're Going, Christopher Columbus?*) has a playful voice that is nothing like the serious one of Diane Stanley (author of *Cleopatra*). Learning to recognize the different techniques writers use to craft their books is like learning to identify different kinds of music.

Experiment

Maybe you usually read only true-life stories. Try other genres to see how authors of fantasy or mystery, for example, write with their unique voices. You may find inspiration in how Kate DiCamillo (author of *The Tale of Despereaux*) crafted this fantasy novel whose heroes include a mouse and rat. You might discover writing tips while reading the adventures of Sherlock Holmes, the hero created by mystery writer Arthur Conan Doyle.

Writers' voices

Look at the kinds of words the following authors use. Do they use lots of adjectives? What about the length and rhythm of their sentences? Which style do you prefer to read?

CASE STUDY

Biographer Diane Stanley began acquiring her writer's voice before she even learned how to write. As a preschooler, Stanley dictated stories to her mother, who wrote them down for her. The young girl drew pictures to illustrate these tales. Today Stanley is a trained artist who often illustrates the books she writes.

Tonya Bolden

Aim high! Stand tall! Be strong!—and do! These ideals were sown in the soul of young Maritcha Remond Lyons, a child of New York City's striving class of blacks in the mid-1800s.
Tonya Bolden, *Maritcha: A Nineteenth-Century American Girl*

Kathleen Krull

No one expected such a tiny girl to have a first birthday. In Clarksville, Tennessee, in 1940, life for a baby who weighed just over four pounds at birth was sure to be limited. But most babies didn't have nineteen older brothers and sisters to watch over them. Most babies didn't have a mother who knew home remedies and a father who worked several jobs. Most babies weren't Wilma Rudolph.
Kathleen Krull, *Wilma Unlimited: How Wilma Rudolph Became the World's Fastest Runner*

Jean Fritz

Before King George the Third was either king or the Third, he was just plain George, a bashful boy who blushed easily. His toes turned in when he walked, and his teachers nagged him about being lazy. Now, of course, as everyone knows, a king should not blush or turn in his toes or be lazy, but George didn't think much about being a king.
Jean Fritz, *Can't You Make Them Behave, King George?*

James Cross Giblin

Out over the Atlantic, Charles looked down on a sea filled with huge, craggy icebergs. Soon fog materialized, thin at first, then thickening until it hid both the ocean and the icebergs. He climbed slowly above the fog, wanting to keep the sky and its stars in view. But the cloud level kept rising, too. Soon he was playing hide-and-seek with the hazy upper clouds and the half dozen or so stars he could still see.
James Cross Giblin, *Charles A. Lindbergh: A Human Hero*

GET YOUR FACTS STRAIGHT

Your first step is to create a timeline for the life of your biography subject. This will help you focus on which events, places, and other people to research further. If you have chosen a famous person, begin your timeline by looking up your subject in an encyclopedia, at the library, or on the Internet. If you plan to write the life story of a community or family member, looking through family records and interviewing that person might be useful for creating this timeline.

Now it's your turn

Matters of life and death

Draw a long vertical line on a sheet of paper. On one side of this line write down every year your subject was alive. On the other side, mark off the years linked to this person's major life events: the year of his or her birth, and when he or she started school, began a job, married, had children, and died. Of course, also list this person's noteworthy achievements and any failures.

Now do some more research on this time period. Go back to the timeline and use a different color ink to add in the important historical events that occurred then—such as wars, natural disasters, or inventions of new technology—and had an impact on your subject's life.

A good biography is much more than just a list of dates and facts. Spice up your work by asking questions—in your research or during an interview—that explore the subject's thoughts and feelings.

Tips and Techniques

Use a tape recorder or take notes during an interview to preserve the information you hear. Not everyone is comfortable being tape recorded, so be certain to ask about this at the beginning of the interview.

FACTS COME TO LIFE

Now it's your turn

Add the spice of life

Look or ask for answers to questions such as these to make dry facts come to life:

- Who had the greatest influence on you as you were growing up? Who influences you today?
- What were your favorite activities?
- When did you first fall in love?
- What was your narrowest escape?
- What was your biggest mistake?
- What do you feel have been your greatest achievements?
- What scares you the most?
- What would you like included in your obituary?

Tips and Techniques
When you write about a living person or someone who has died recently, think about what you will do if you discover any secrets. Will you reveal them? How will this person or surviving family members feel if you do reveal family secrets? How will you handle any negative reactions from them?

CASE STUDY

Some life stories are so intimately connected that they are best told together. For this reason, Russell Freedman wrote about the Wright Brothers (right) together. James Cross Giblin, looking at the assassination of Abraham Lincoln, penned *Good Brother, Bad Brother: The Story of Edwin Booth and John Wilkes Booth.*

Tips and Techniques

Be accurate. Biographers may be sued for libel if they write false statements that damage someone's reputation. Kathleen Krull jokingly remarks that one reason she prefers to write about "dead people" is that "they can't sue for talking about things like underwear" or other intimate details.

GET THE PICTURE

Photographs or paintings of where your biography subject lived will inspire you as you re-create the setting for readers. Using photos and paintings is especially important if your subject lived long ago or in a faraway place. You may not be able to journey through time or visit a distant land, but your imagination can take you and your readers anywhere.

Biographer Elizabeth Partridge was not even born when folk singer Woody Guthrie traveled through America in the 1930s. Yet her words capture the sights and sounds he experienced as he left the dry, dusty Southwest and reached California. In *This Land Was Made for You and Me: The Life and Songs of Woody Guthrie*, Partridge notes:

Spring was coming, and Woody couldn't believe the intense greens of all the new foliage bursting out everywhere. It was almost painfully bright to look at after the drab grays and browns of the Dust Bowl. Even the air smelled moist and delicious and full of promise.

Now it's your turn

Live in the moment

Examine a photograph or painting of a place that was important in your subject's life. Notice all the details, using a magnifying glass if necessary. Now write a 100-word description of that place as though you were right there. What do you see or smell? How hot or cold is it? What else do you feel as you brush up against objects or people in this setting? Who else is there? What kinds of feelings do the expressions on their faces suggest? What noises or conversations do you hear?

CASE STUDY

Russell Freedman looked at more than 4,000 photographs online when he researched his biography of singer Marian Anderson, *The Voice That Challenged a Nation: Marian Anderson and the Struggle for Equal Rights*. Freedman found most of them at one university Web site. The author usually selects about 140 photographs to inspire and illustrate his award-winning books, such as *Lincoln: A Photobiography*.

Tips and Techniques
Many museums and government agencies have Web sites displaying their collections of photographs and paintings. Use these great resources for your setting and possible illustrations.

Of course, you may already be familiar with settings important in the life of a community leader or family member. You may even be lucky enough to visit one of the settings in your biography for the very first time. Though it isn't essential, many professional biographers try to include travel in their research into someone's life. Russell Freedman visited China several times while he wrote *Confucius: The Golden Rule*. He planned one trip to coincide with a community celebration of this ancient philosopher's birthday.

Tips and Techniques
Complete the first draft of a book before traveling to its settings. "Otherwise," as Russell Freedman says, "you don't know what you're looking for."

FOLLOW THE MAP

Books sometimes include maps to help readers understand the geographical relationships and events described in their pages. James Cross Giblin's *The Life and Death of Adolf Hitler* contains several maps of Europe. They demonstrate the spread of Nazism during World War II. A map may be another tool to help you figure out and communicate the settings of your subject's life.

Now it's your turn

Following life's highways and byways

Use the Internet, an encyclopedia, or an atlas to find a map of a city or community important in your subject's life. Use what you have learned about this person to figure out distances here. For instance, how far did he or she walk or ride each day from home to school or work? How far was it to visit family or friends? How long did these trips take? Think about the sights and sounds your subject probably experienced along the way. How did changing seasons affect these routes and experiences?

Use this map information as you look again at pictures of these settings. Now write 100 words describing what your subject experienced during one typical trip. Help your readers to see, hear, smell, feel, and even taste what your subject probably noticed then.

CASE STUDY

Author-illustrator Diane Stanley has two jobs when setting the scene for readers. As she notes, her own drawings as well as her words have to "reconstruct" the "cast of characters and the costumes they wear … the food they eat, the carriages on the street, and the look of the landscape." For many years, she did all this through research, but Stanley has recently begun to travel to locations. "It's pretty amazing," she says, "to stand in the very house where Joan of Arc was born!" (above)

CHAPTER 3: CHARACTERS

DISCOVER YOUR HERO

Whether you chose a real-life hero, an ordinary person, or even a villain to write about, you now have the job of making readers know and care about this person. To have this connection, they need to understand what your subject thought and felt at different points in life.

Build a picture

If your subject lived long ago or far away, you may need to give readers information about that time and place. Elizabeth Partridge builds a picture of how hard life was for Woody Guthrie and other Americans during the Great Depression. Dorothea Lange, herself the subject of a biography by Partridge, photographed the Depression's suffering families (left). Russell Freedman pictures the problems Confucius and other scholars in ancient China faced before the invention of paper.

People stood in long lines just to get a bowl of soup and a cup of weak coffee. Homeless people camped out in parks, under highway overpasses and garbage dumps, or slept in their cars.
Elizabeth Partridge, *This Land Was Made for You and Me: The Life and Songs of Woody Guthrie*

Books back then (in Confucius' time) were bulky and clumsy. Copies were few. They were inscribed with a stylus on strips of bamboo bound together by leather cords, resembling Venetian blinds.
Russell Freedman, *Confucius: The Golden Rule*

Now it's your turn

Life's historic moments

Look again at your timeline. Can you build a picture of the important historic events listed there? Quickly write a paragraph about one event. Now read it to see if it contains interesting details. Decide if you need to do more research about major events that touched your subject's life.

Heroic qualities

Is your subject physically brave, or does his or her courage rest in strength of will? What other heroic qualities does this person have? As Tonya Bolden demonstrates in *Maritcha: A Nineteenth-Century American Girl*, even little-known people may fight and win heroic struggles in their daily lives. Do your subject's heroic qualities outweigh the negative ones? In *Charles A. Lindbergh: A Human Hero*, James Cross Giblin suggests that this is so. However, Giblin shows in *The Life and Death of Adolf Hitler* that this dictator's strengths were insignificant compared to the death and destruction he caused.

TELL YOUR SUBJECT'S WEAKNESSES AND PROBLEMS

The Life and Death of Adolf Hitler focuses on the great harm this dictator's ambitions caused. Yet James Cross Giblin gives readers insight into Hitler by describing the problems he had as a child, when his father frequently beat him with a whip. Giblin shows how Hitler was disappointed and frustrated as a teenager when he failed to get into art school.

Elizabeth Partridge tells how Woody Guthrie often went hungry as a boy, yet as an adult, he frequently abandoned his first wife and young children.

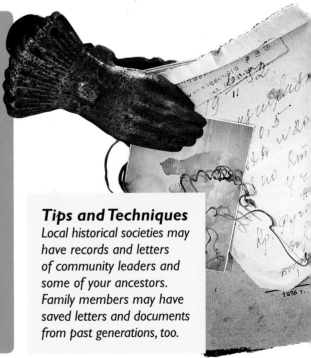

CASE STUDIES

Tonya Bolden was inspired to write *Maritcha: A Nineteenth-Century American Girl* after she discovered an unpublished memoir by Maritcha Remond Lyons. Bolden quotes from and gives credit to this document, which Maritcha titled *Memories of Yesterday: All of Which I Saw and Part of Which I Was.*

Elizabeth Partridge drew upon autobiographies that Woody Guthrie wrote.

Tips and Techniques
Local historical societies may have records and letters of community leaders and some of your ancestors. Family members may have saved letters and documents from past generations, too.

Build character

Help readers see your subject. Use your own vivid words. Add the eloquent descriptions of others who knew this person as well as personal descriptions made by the subject. In his biography of Abraham Lincoln, Russell Freedman notes that:

> *At first glance, most people thought he was homely. Lincoln thought so too, referring once to his "poor, lean, lank face." As a young man he was sensitive about his gawky looks, but in time, he learned to laugh at himself.*
> Russell Freedman, *Lincoln: A Photobiography*

Now it's your turn

Walk in someone else's shoes

Close your eyes. Take three minutes to think about the worst problem your biography subject faced as a child or young adult. What would you have felt or done in that situation? How similar or different would your reactions be? Open your eyes and begin to write. For the next seven minutes, let your ideas gush out onto the page. Use this new awareness of a difficult situation when you write about your subject's weaknesses and problems.

Tips and Techniques

Find out if your subject kept a journal or diary or perhaps wrote an autobiography. Use these to gain insight into the person's thoughts and feelings.

WHO CAUSES PROBLEMS?

Your subject may face problems caused by other people. Or this person's difficulties may be the result of larger situations beyond anyone's control—illness, war, or natural disasters. Identify the different sources of your subject's problems and bring these to life for the reader.

Woody Guthrie's mother, Nora, had a brain disorder called Huntington's disease that caused her to be unpredictably violent:

> *One moment Nora would treat her children well, then something awful would come over her. Her face would twitch and her lips would draw up into a snarl. Spit would run out of her mouth and her arms would jerk uncontrollably. A screeching mutter would start in her throat and then build up until she was screaming, "God, I want to die! I want to die. Now! Now!" Then she would smash dishes and throw furniture around the house.*
> Elizabeth Partridge, *This Land Was Made for You and Me: The Life and Songs of Woody Guthrie*

What is the motive?

People commit evil deeds for different reasons. If there are villains in this life story, are they motivated by greed? By fear? By the desire for power? Or do they believe that their acts are not really evil at all?

Villainous acts

Actor John Wilkes Booth assassinated Abraham Lincoln in what he believed was a patriotic act supporting the Confederacy. After this brutal deed in Ford's Theatre, Booth jumped onto the stage:

> *Relishing his last moment in the spotlight, John raised himself to his full height, and a few audience members recognized him. He fixed his gaze on the state box, brandished the bloody knife, and shouted the Latin words "Sic semper tyrannis!" ("Thus always to tyrants!") Some thought they also heard him say, "The South is avenged!"*
> James Cross Giblin, *Good Brother, Bad Brother: The Story of Edwin Booth and John Wilkes Booth*

Hitler's army slaughtered all people whom the Nazis considered enemies and inferiors, not just soldiers. In Russia, for example:

> *In each Soviet village they came to, the special-duty troops rounded up all the Jews who lived there and marched them out into the countryside, along with the Communist leaders of the community. There, without any trial or other proceeding, the Jewish and Communist prisoners were forced to dig a ditch. Then they were lined up and shot, their corpses falling backward into the ditch they had just dug.*
> James Cross Giblin, *The Life and Death of Adolf Hitler*

Develop your supporting cast

Be sure to add details or descriptions that will bring minor characters in the biography to life. Just a sentence or two or even a few words can make an enormous difference. Russell Freedman describes Marian Anderson's vocal coach:

> *Boghetti was short, stocky, and dynamic, a demanding teacher with a vast store of knowledge about vocal technique and a stern manner with his students.*
> Russell Freedman, *The Voice That Challenged a Nation: Marian Anderson and the Struggle for Equal Rights*

Elizabeth Partridge describes a class that photographer Dorothea Lange took:

> *It was taught by Clarence White, a small, gentle, inarticulate photographer. He had a fine, absolute sense of what was beautiful and struggled to teach his students how to capture it on film.*
> Elizabeth Partridge, *Restless Spirit: The Life and Work of Dorothea Lange*

Well-written characters will breathe life into any biography you write!

CHOOSE A POINT OF VIEW

Who will tell the story of this biography—someone who knows everything that happened and what everyone in it thought and felt? Perhaps you believe the subject of your biography would be the best person to tell at least some of its events. Or you might decide that these events should be told from the viewpoints of several of the people who experienced them. Before you write the biography, you must choose a point of view or points of view for it.

Omniscient viewpoint

Biographies set in the distant past are often told from the all-seeing and all-knowing—the omniscient—point of view. This permits the writer to include explanations of settings and events that readers might not know. It also permits the writer to mention any gaps in our knowledge about events that occurred long ago. Describing the death of Cleopatra (right) in ancient Egypt, Diane Stanley writes:

No one knows exactly how she died, except that she must have taken poison in some form. Many believe that she had arranged for a poisonous asp to be smuggled in, hidden among the figs.
Diane Stanley, *Cleopatra*

Tips and Techniques
Use phrases such as "As far as we know" and "It is said that" to introduce information that can no longer be proven true. Russell Freedman frequently uses these phrases in his biography of the ancient Chinese philosopher, Confucius.

| GETTING STARTED | SETTING THE SCENE | CHARACTERS | VIEWPOINT |

First-person viewpoint

The first-person viewpoint, using "I" or "we," permits readers to hear someone's inner thoughts or actual speech. A responsible biographer uses first-person viewpoint only for words that records show the subject or other characters actually spoke or wrote. The biographer places quotation marks around these words or sentences. For a full picture of someone's life, biographers usually combine the first-person viewpoint with others, such as an omniscient or third-person viewpoint. Russell Freedman combines viewpoints in his account of Marian Anderson's history-making concert at the Lincoln Memorial:

> Anderson faced the now hushed and expectant crowd that stretched across the Mall from the base of the Lincoln Memorial all the way to the Washington Monument. Directly behind her, the great Lincoln Memorial was filled with shadow in the late-afternoon light. And the statue of Lincoln looked almost ready to speak.
>
> "There seemed to be people as far as the eye could see," Anderson recalled. "I had a feeling that a great wave of good will poured out from these people, almost engulfing me. And when I stood up to sing ... I felt for a moment as though I were choking. For a desperate second I thought that the words, well as I knew them, would not come. I sang, I don't know how."
> Russell Freedman, *The Voice That Challenged a Nation: Marian Anderson and the Struggle for Equal Rights*

THIRD-PERSON VIEWPOINT

The third-person viewpoint follows the experiences, thoughts, and feelings of one character, who knows what other characters think or feel only by interacting with them. The biographer refers to this narrator, who may be the subject of the biography, by the person's name and "he" or "she." Elizabeth Partridge uses third-person viewpoint, combined with first-person viewpoint, in her biography of photographer Dorothea Lange:

Dorothea was fourteen when she stood in the back parlor with her mother's friend, staring out the window. It was washday, and laundry hung from the high line strung across the backyard. The wash flapped and billowed in the breeze, making vivid patterns against the late afternoon sky. A rusty squeaking from the line filled the air.

"To me, that is beautiful," Dorothea said, breaking her reverie.

The friend replied, "To you, everything is beautiful."

That surprised Dorothea. "I thought everyone saw everything I saw and didn't talk about it." It also helped her. "It made me aware that maybe I had eyesight."

Elizabeth Partridge, *Restless Spirit: The Life and Work of Dorothea Lange*

Multiple viewpoints

Using multiple points of view adds drama to a biography. James Cross Giblin follows the intense thoughts and experiences of assassin John Wilkes Booth throughout the middle chapters of *Good Brother, Bad Brother*. Giblin focuses on his actor brother Edwin Booth in the opening and concluding chapters of the book.

In *Carver: A Life in Poems*, poet Marilyn Nelson depicts the life of scientist and agriculture professor George Washington Carver (right) in 44 poems, written from more than 30 different points of view. These poems permit Nelson to show not only the accomplishments of this former slave, but also the wide range of reactions he drew from people of different backgrounds.

One of Carver's African-American college students unreasonably dislikes him:

> *Talking all those big words, quoting poems at you*
> *in that womanish voice. So high and mighty,*
> *he must think he's white.*
> Marilyn Nelson, "My People" in *Carver: A Life in Poems*

A farmer, however, praised Carver in his poorly spelled letter to him:

> *What maid my cotton grow? It do fele grate*
> *to see the swet off your brow com to bloom.*
> *I want to now what maid my miracle.*
> *Your humble servint, (name illegible)*
> Marilyn Nelson, "From an Alabama Farmer" in *Carver: A Life in Poems*

Your choice of points of view helps readers get the point of your biography.

Now it's your turn

Seeing other points of view

Experiment with your choice of viewpoints. Think about your subject's greatest achievement or failure. Take 10 minutes to write a paragraph about this event from his or her third-person viewpoint. Then write another paragraph telling this story from the viewpoint of the subject's relative, friend, or even enemy. Which completed paragraph is more interesting to read? Do you have any researched first-person words you can add to this paragraph? Include these or substitute them for some of your own. How does the addition of a first-person voice make your paragraph more or less interesting?

TELL YOUR STORY'S STORY

As the biography takes shape in your mind, it is a good idea to describe it in a paragraph or two. This is called a synopsis. If someone asked, "What is the biography about?" these paragraphs would be the answer. An editor often wants to see a synopsis of a biography before accepting it for publication.

Study back cover blurbs

Studying the information on the back cover of a book—called the blurb—will help you write an effective synopsis. A good blurb contains a brief summary of a book's content. It also gives the tone of the book—whether it is serious or funny. Most important of all, the blurb makes readers want to open the book and read it cover-to-cover! That is certainly true of this blurb:

> *Hitler's murderous actions left their mark, in one way or another, on everyone who lived in the latter two-thirds of the twentieth century. What sort of man could plan and carry out such horrendous schemes? How was he able to win support for his deadly ventures? And why did no one try to stop him until it was almost too late?*
> James Cross Giblin, *The Life and Death of Adolf Hitler*

Sometimes an intriguing quotation makes a dramatic blurb, as it does on the back cover of Russell Freedman's *The Voice That Challenged a Nation: Marian Anderson and the Struggle for Equal Rights:*

> *"She wore the glorious crown of her voice with the grace of an empress and changed the lives of many through the subtle force of her spirit and demeanor. If the planet Earth could sing, I think it would sound something like Marian Anderson."*
> Jessye Norman, opera and concert singer, *The New York Times Magazine*

Make a story map

One way to plan the biography is to think of it the way filmmakers prepare a movie. Before the cameras start shooting, they must know the main story episodes. They must also map out the plot (the sequence of events) in a series of sketches called storyboards. You can do this for your biography. The blurb and timeline you wrote will help you here.

Write a chapter synopsis

Another way to plan the biography is to write a chapter synopsis. Look at the timeline of your subject's life. Group major events there into five to eight categories, such as childhood, career, marriage, successes, and setbacks. Use each of these categories as a chapter. Following a chapter synopsis as an outline is one helpful way to keep on track as you write.

Now it's your turn

Lights! Camera! Action!

Reread your blurb. Use it to identify the most important events on the timeline of your subject's life. You are now ready to sketch the "scenes" for the biography's storyboards. Under each sketched scene, jot down brief notes about what you will mention about this event. Use this series of storyboards as a helpful outline as you write the biography. If your biography has chapters, each scene may be a separate chapter. Perhaps two or more scenes will fit together well in one chapter.

Tips and Techniques

Some interesting or important information may not fit smoothly into the biography's sequence of events. Put these nuggets of information into sidebars, or short pieces of separate text.

CASE STUDY

In *Leonardo: Beautiful Dreamer*, Robert Byrd frequently uses sidebars to explain the many interests of Renaissance genius Leonardo da Vinci. These sidebars include information about science, engineering, art, astronomy, and language. They also give further information about the people da Vinci knew and the places where he lived.

BAIT THE HOOK

Now that you have planned your biography, how will you catch and keep the reader's attention? You might choose a fascinating first sentence to reel readers into your work.

Your attention-grabbing sentence could be dark and mysterious, if this style matches your subject. James Cross Giblin makes such a match with this first sentence:

> *Edwin Booth often had premonitions that something bad was going to happen.*
> James Cross Giblin, *Good Brother, Bad Brother: The Story of Edwin Booth and John Wilkes Booth*

The sentence could be playful and humorous, if this style fits your subject's life. That is how Kathleen Krull begins her biography of Dr. Seuss:

> *Once upon a time, there lived a boy who feasted on books and was wild about animals.*
> Kathleen Krull, *The Boy on Fairfield Street: How Ted Geisel Grew Up to Become Dr. Seuss*

The style of the opening sentence should fit not only your subject's life but also the voice you use throughout the biography.

Now it's your turn

Lively beginnings

In the library or a bookstore, look at the opening chapters of different biographies. See which techniques they use to hook readers. Which method do you enjoy reading? Which method do you think you will use? Brainstorm sentences and think of dramatic events you could use to begin the biography you are planning. Write out several openings to discover the one you find most satisfying.

Hook your readers

You might decide to hook readers with an entire chapter filled with excitement and drama. Some biographies begin with the subject's biggest achievement rather than his or her birth. That is how Russell Freedman begins his biography of Marian Anderson. Its first chapter is titled "Easter Sunday, April 9, 1939." This is the date of Anderson's history-making concert. The chapter describes Anderson and the thousands of people who gathered to hear her sing in Washington, D.C., that day.

It is also how Freedman begins his biography of the Wright brothers. Its dramatic first chapter, titled "What Amos Root Saw," begins this way:

> *No one had ever seen what Amos Root saw on that September afternoon in 1904. Standing in a cow pasture near Dayton, Ohio, he looked up and watched a flying machine circle in the sky above him. He could see the bold pilot lying facedown on the lower wing, staring straight ahead as he steered the craft to a landing in the grass. The pilot was Wilbur Wright. He and his brother Orville had built the machine themselves in the workroom of their bicycle shop. Now they were testing it out at a farmer's field called Huffman Prairie.*
> Russell Freedman, *The Wright Brothers: How They Invented the Airplane*

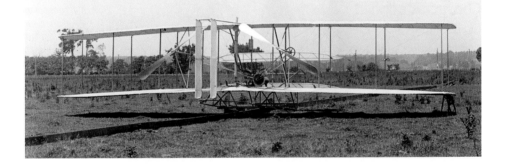

Tips and Techniques

Is your biography set in the distant past or a faraway place? If so, consider writing a preface or opening author's note for it. This extra introduction contains background material about the subject's time and place that may be unfamiliar to readers. Diane Stanley begins both Cleopatra *and* Saladin: Noble Prince of Islam *in this way.*

BUILD THE SUSPENSE

After your exciting opening, do not let the excitement die. Keep and build suspense for your readers by crafting the biography in ways that emphasize the dramatic events in your subject's life.

Thrills and chills

Keep your readers on the edge of their seats by hinting about unusual, unexpected, or unpleasant events that will occur in the future. This writing technique—called foreshadowing—will have readers eagerly turning pages to find out what happens next. Tonya Bolden uses foreshadowing when she writes:

> *All the while that Maritcha kept hush-hush about her parents' heroism, she never imagined that one day she would be on the run and a refugee. This happened amid the catastrophe that hit New York City shortly after Maritcha turned fifteen, during the sweltering days of mid-July 1863.* Tonya Bolden, *Maritcha: A Nineteenth-Century American Girl*

Character conflict

Do not ignore the struggles and setbacks that even successful people experience. Which people or situations posed problems for your subject? Did this person get into any arguments, fights, or feuds? Whether these conflicts were in someone's personal or professional life, be certain to include them as part of the biography's story line. Remember that people often experience more than one conflict at a time. The narrative that you are writing may have subplots as well as a main plot.

Now it's your turn

Life's struggles

Examine the storyboards or chapters you are using to organize the biography. For each one, make notes to indicate any conflicts your subject experienced during that event or time. Maintain suspense by including these conflicts as you write this life story. Include any subplot struggles as well as conflicts related to the main plot.

Cliff-hangers

Sometimes television shows end just as the main characters are in great danger—standing at the very edge of a high cliff, so to speak. Or the show may end with a character about to make an important decision. Viewers tune in to the next episode just to find out what happens. To keep readers involved, end your chapters in similarly suspenseful ways. For example, James Cross Giblin concludes one of his chapters about John Wilkes Booth (right) with this cliff-hanger:

> *John did not answer her letter right away. He had other, more pressing matters on his mind, including a bold new plan to kidnap the president.*
> James Cross Giblin, *Good Brother, Bad Brother: The Story of Edwin Booth and John Wilkes Booth*

CASE STUDY

James Cross Giblin recognizes it is challenging to write lively text while sticking closely to the facts. He says, "When I'm researching the subject, I always look for the story line in the material. Every nonfiction topic has one, whether it is the aggressive moves Adolf Hitler made in his rise to power, or the way John Wilkes Booth plotted first to kidnap and then murder Abraham Lincoln."

Tips and Techniques

Write chapter titles that not only indicate content but create suspense and hold reader interest. Russell Freedman does this in his biography of Lincoln with chapter titles such as "This Dreadful War" and "Who Is Dead in the White House?"

END WITH A BANG

Write an ending that leaves readers still thinking about your subject and the life story you've told. It may seem that someone's death would be the logical place to end a biography, but there are other effective ways to "wrap up" a life story. Of course, these techniques are particularly important to keep in mind if your subject is still alive!

What if?

Asking and answering a "What if?" question about the subject's life is one intriguing way to conclude a biography. What if the subject had never lived?

What if this person had made a different choice at an important turning point? What if events had turned out differently at that critical point? Diane Stanley uses this method to end her biography of Cleopatra with a bang:

In a world where women had little power, she had fought to control the destiny of nations. And if she had succeeded in her great venture, it would have been Cleopatra and her descendants who ruled the Western world, instead of the emperors of Rome.
Diane Stanley, *Cleopatra*

And life goes on ...

You may even decide to end the biography of someone already dead long before the person died. Focusing on one part of someone's life or on one important event in it is called a biographical sketch or profile. Kathleen Krull's biography of Ted Geisel focuses on his boyhood and ends when he published his first Dr. Seuss works at the age of 22. In an afterword titled "On Beyond Fairfield Street," Krull summarizes in detail the rest of Geisel's long, productive life.

What are the consequences?

Explaining the consequences of your subject's life—the impact this person has had on others or the world—is another effective way to end a biography. Your subject might have helped family members, been a community leader, or played a larger role in national or world affairs. Some biographers like Russell Freedman write an entire final chapter set after a subject's death. In Marian Anderson's biography, Freedman concludes that:

> Anderson's exceptional musical gifts and her uncompromising artistic standards made it possible for her to break through racial barriers. She became a role model, inspiring generations of African American performers who followed her. But it was the strength of her character, her undaunted spirit and unshakable dignity, that transformed her from a singer to an international symbol of progress in the advancement of human rights.
>
> Russell Freedman, *The Voice That Challenged a Nation: Marian Anderson and the Struggle for Equal Rights*

Now it's your turn

Where will it end?
Decide if your biography will be a sketch that focuses on just one part of the subject's life. If you choose to write such a profile, rather than a complete biography, remember that you need to summarize the rest of the subject's life in an afterword.

A personal note

If you had a special reason for choosing your subject, consider including it in an author's note after the end of the biography. In the afterword to her biography of Woody Guthrie, Elizabeth Partridge explains how her interest in the songwriter stemmed from a humiliating event in sixth grade. Partridge sang so badly that for a performance, her music teacher told her to just silently mouth the words to Guthrie's song "This Land Is Your Land!" Sometimes an author's note explains the experiences the biographer had in researching a subject's life. Russell Freedman tells about his adventures in China in his author's note to *Confucius: The Golden Rule*.

MAKE YOUR WORDS WORK

Words are the heart of your biography. They can pump life vigorously into the story or weakly let it die right before the reader's eyes. Choose words wisely to keep the biography in great shape.

A sense of life

Use as many of the five senses as possible to make descriptions come alive. Smell as well as sight help readers experience the work of photographer Dorothea Lange (right).

> *With the darkroom lit only by the soft yellow glow of a "safe light," Dorothea took the negatives from their holders and developed them in baths of sharp-smelling chemicals.*
> Elizabeth Partridge, *Restless Spirit: The Life and Work of Dorothea Lange*

After he moved to Paris to attend school, Louis Braille, who was blind, relied heavily on his other senses. Russell Freedman helps readers experience life as Braille did:

> *From the street below, he could hear the rumble of wheels and the clicking of hooves as carriages rolled past on the cobblestone pavement. A warm breeze swept through the window, carrying memories of spring in his own village. At home, the fields now would feel moist and soft beneath his bare feet. The hills would be fragrant with the smell of new clover.*
> Russell Freedman, *Out of Darkness: The Story of Louis Braille*

By following these examples, you can help readers have a sensational experience as they read your biography.

Use vivid imagery

Bring scenes to life by creating vivid word pictures with metaphors and similes. One of Marilyn Nelson's characters calls young George Washington Carver "a wizard with a washboard." This does not mean that Carver performed magic, but that he did an excellent job washing clothes in this old-fashioned way. This word picture communicates how hard and intensely Carver worked.

Nelson also uses similes to help readers see and feel how the task of sewing relaxed an older Carver. She writes, "The cloth lies on your lap like an infant in a christening gown, as smooth under your palm as your mother's lost skirts." These word pictures of gentle and tender things communicate how sewing soothed Carver.

Tips and Techniques
A metaphor describes something by calling it something else—for instance, a fierce man is a "tiger." A simile describes something by comparing it to something with the word "like" or "as." For example, a dewdrop sparkles like a diamond.

Write to excite

When you write action scenes, excite your readers with your word choice. Replace everyday action words with bold, unusual ones. Have characters race instead of run and leap instead of jump. Tonya Bolden uses vivid action words as well as a metaphor to describe a riot:

Telegraph poles—hacked down! Rail tracks—yanked up! Wooden fences—ripped apart! With planks, crowbars, bricks, broadaxes, knives, and guns, a whirlwind of mobs went wild.
Tonya Bolden, *Maritcha: A Nineteenth-Century American Girl*

Now it's your turn

Lively words

By yourself or with a friend, make a list of 10 everyday actions words such as walk or fall. Then have fun brainstorming at least four unusual substitutes for each word. Perhaps someone would plunge instead of fall. Use a dictionary or thesaurus for extra help. Make every word count. Needless words are like extra pounds—they weigh your writing down when you want your biography fit and trim.

IN THEIR OWN WORDS

Unlike writers of fiction, biographers do not make up words and put them into the mouths of their characters. Every word that appears in quotation marks in a well-written biography comes from a reliable source—such as letters, diaries, or interviews—and was actually spoken or written by the person being quoted. Using someone's own words is a great way to give readers a sense of that individual's personality along with information.

Quality quotations

Dorothea Lange's use of simile gave insight into her beliefs and feelings:

> Dorothea was adamant about having enough time for her work. "Artists are controlled by the life that beats in them, like the ocean beats on the shore," she said. And the desire beating within her was the urge to be out on the streets, photographing.
> Elizabeth Partridge, *Restless Spirit: The Life and Work of Dorothea Lange*

Charles Lindbergh used metaphor and simile to describe his experience of flying high:

> "Trees became bushes; barns, toys; cows turned into rabbits as we climbed," Lindbergh later wrote. "All the country around Lincoln lay like a relief map below."
> James Cross Giblin, *Charles A. Lindbergh: A Human Hero*

Tips and Techniques

Select quotations that vividly communicate someone's mood or personality. If you can paraphrase the quotation without losing that extra flavor, you probably should use your own words instead.

Chief Sitting Bull (right) was quietly eloquent about the Battle of the Little Bighorn:

> *"All my warriors were brave and knew no fear,"* Sitting Bull said later. *"The soldiers who were killed were brave men, too, but they had no chance to fight or run away. They were surrounded too closely by our many warriors. ... We did not go out of our own country to kill them. They came to kill us and got killed themselves."*
> Russell Freedman, *The Life and Death of Crazy Horse*

India's Prime Minister Indira Gandhi could be wise and funny at the same time. To be effective:

> *"A Prime Minister must always be a little upset,"* she lamented.
> Kathleen Krull, "Tiger Among Monkeys: Indira Gandhi," in *Lives of Extraordinary Women: Rulers, Rebels (and What the Neighbors Thought)*

Tips and Techniques

Use say, said, or wrote to introduce quotations. You can sometimes substitute words such as complained, whispered, or shouted for variety and when they suit the situation.

Now it's your turn

Who said that?

Look through your notes and research materials. Find three to five quotations that communicate the personality of the person who spoke or wrote these words. This person could be your subject; his or her friend, family member, or co-worker; a reporter or historian writing about the subject; or even an enemy. Add these quotations to the biography. Try paraphrasing each quotation to be certain it has enough special flavor to be worthwhile.

USE DRAMATIC DIALOGUE

Reliable sources—such as interviews, diaries, historical records, and autobiographies—may provide real-life dialogue that you can use to write your biography.

Dialogue lets your readers hear what people in the biography said in their own words. Conversations between people are a great storytelling device—they give information, create a mood, and add color. People may have talked quietly, argued bitterly, or comforted each other tenderly. Dialogue communicates and adds emotion to the events in any life story. It is a way to show, rather than merely tell, about an event.

Follow convention

Dialogue is usually written down according to certain rules. Each new speaker begins a new paragraph. You already know that what a person actually said is enclosed in quotation marks, followed or preceded by a tag such as "he said" or "she said." Sometimes, to give the sense of a real conversation, writers place these tags in the middle of a sentence. This placement adds another rhythm to the conversation, making it more lifelike. Sometimes, biographers use information from their sources to add descriptions of gestures, faces, and actions to a dialogue.

Listen in to history

This conversation shows how daily life in poor Southern communities inspired Woody Guthrie's music:

> *Rambling around town one day,*
> *Woody was passing the barbershop*
> *when he heard a man playing the harmon-*
> *ica. Woody was immediately mesmerized.*
> *"That's the lonesomest piece of music I ever run*
> *into," he said. "Where in the world did you learn it?"*
> *"I just lay here and listen to the railroad whistle," the man*
> *replied. "Whatever it say, I say too."*
> Elizabeth Partridge, *This Land Was Made for You and Me: The*
> *Life and Songs of Woody Guthrie*

AMERICAN
HISTORICAL
DOCUMENTS

REAL LIFE WORDS

In the dialogue you write, keep the slang and grammar mistakes that are sometimes part of everyday speech. Such lifelike dialogue helps readers hear the social class and regional background of the speakers.

This dialogue shows how a servant brought news of hunted assassin John Wilkes Booth to his sister Asia:

The federal guard allowed him to enter, and as soon as Asia saw the man standing nervously by the center table in her room, she guessed what he had come to tell her.
"Is it over?" she asked.
"Yes, madam," the man answered without raising his eyes.
"Taken?"
"Yes."
"Dead?"
"Yes, madam."
Her heart beat like strong machinery, Asia wrote later, but she did not cry.
James Cross Giblin, *Good Brother, Bad Brother: The Story of Edwin Booth and John Wilkes Booth*

Now it's your turn

Be dramatic

Look through your research materials and notes. Find a conversation that captures a mood as well as conveys information. Include all or part of this conversation at the appropriate point in the biography, using tags to introduce the material and following the paragraph rules.

Now it's your turn

Say that again!

Try other ways of introducing quotations and dialogue in your biography. Use tags in the middle of a sentence or between sentences. Remove all tags to see if such back-and-forth dialogue remains clear and seems more dramatic. See which technique works best at different points in your book.

BEAT WRITER'S BLOCK

Even famous writers sometimes get stuck for words or ideas. This is called writer's block. If you have been following the writer's golden rule (writing regularly and often), you already have some ways to battle writer's block. Here are some of its causes and other weapons to use.

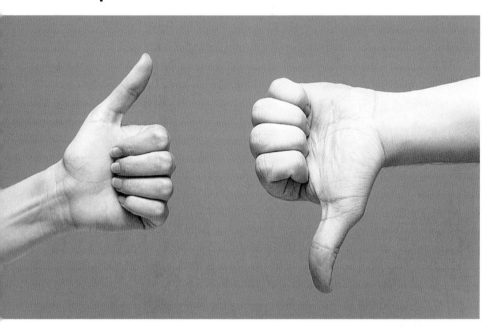

Your inner critic

Do not listen to that inner voice that might whisper negative ideas about your writing. All writers try out and then throw away some of their efforts. Pam Munoz Ryan may revise a manuscript up to 10 times before she ever submits it to an editor. After her editor sees a manuscript, Ryan often revises her work another three or four times. She tells young authors that writing is just "like anything else in life, the harder you work the luckier you get. The more you practice, the better you get."

No ideas

Have you run out of ideas? Be inspired by the efforts of other biographers. Look at biographies of people who lived when or where your subject did or who had similar success. See the different ways that many biographers have written about the same famous person. For instance, both Pam Munoz Ryan and Russell Freedman have written the life story of Marian Anderson (right).

Tips and Techniques

Don't let writer's block get in your way. Get inspiration and new ideas by examining several biographies of one famous person.

A WRITERS' GROUP

Writing may seem lonely. Some writers take heart by sharing their works-in-progress with other writers. They meet regularly in person or over the Internet with "writing buddies." These critique groups help fight writer's block by sharing ideas, experiences, and even goals. Often members agree to bring a specific number of new pages to each meeting.

Now it's your turn

Live it up with other writers

Start a writer's group with other writers, or partner up with a writing buddy. Set a regular meeting time and place, and talk about how much new work you will bring to meetings.

A change of pace

Defeat writer's block by changing your writing habits. If you normally brainstorm sitting still, try walking instead. If you usually like quiet while you write, add music to your biography-writing zone. If you write at the computer, try pen and paper. Vary your writing habits for each stage of the process. Russell Freedman handwrites each of his books but uses a computer to type finished drafts. After he prints out a copy, Freedman uses a pencil for corrections and revisions.

Now it's your turn

Step lively!

Don't sit still for writer's block. Change your writing habits to defeat it. Sometimes even a very simple change of pace helps. Take a break with a walk outdoors, a quick household chore, or an errand to the store. A short time away from writing may be all you need.

NOW WHAT?

Congratulations! Completing a biography is a wonderful achievement. You have learned a lot about writing and probably about yourself, too. You are now ready to take the next step in a lifetime filled with writing adventures.

Another biography?

Perhaps while researching this biography you discovered another person whose life fascinates you. Diane Stanley decided to write about the artist Michelangelo (left) while she was working on a biography of Leonardo da Vinci. She says she got an intriguing "whiff of Michelangelo's personality, since the two men knew and disliked each other." Stanley also discovered that Michelangelo had "led a really interesting life." Another biography may be your next writing project.

Write related fiction

Perhaps one of the settings or events in your subject's life caught your imagination. You may have wondered what other people thought, felt, and acted like then. These thoughts might be just the inspiration you need to write a work of fiction.

Now it's your turn

Make a story come alive

Brainstorm your next story with pen and paper. List five events or settings from your subject's life on a piece of paper. For the next 10 minutes, let your ideas about people who might have been involved in each event or place flow onto the page. What problems did they face? How could they have solved them? Do not worry about complete sentences or punctuation. When you are done, you may have found the characters or plot for your next story or biography.

LEARN FROM THE AUTHORS

You can learn a great deal from the advice of successful writers. Almost all will tell you that hard work and occasional failure are part of the writing lifestyle. Yet even though few writers earn enough from their books to make a living, they value their ability to create and communicate through written words.

Russell Freedman

Russell Freedman (left) first believed he could be a writer when his fifth-grade teacher praised his work. Later, being a news reporter sharpened his skills.

Freedman avoids feeling "stuck" as he writes by taking long walks through a park. He says, "I love to write, however painful it is. Even when you're doing a first draft, you know you're going to get to the third draft when it really becomes exhilarating."

James Cross Giblin

James Cross Giblin (right) worked for many years as an editor, guiding other writers, before he began to write himself. He has published more than 20 books. Giblin advises young authors to keep a diary or journal to record events in everyday life. He says, "Try to capture the flavor of what happened and how you felt about it through vivid description and fresh turns of phrase. Writing a journal for an author is like exercise for an athlete. It helps keep you limber and in shape."

Kathleen Krull

Kathleen Krull expects crafting a book to take time. She is not discouraged even when—as happened with her biography of Cesar Chavez—"only one sentence from the first draft makes it into the final book." She recommends that young writers keep diaries or journals. She started to do this "in sixth grade, but didn't really get the hang of it till high school." Her final "words of wisdom" to young writers are, "Turn off the TV and read a book."

Kathleen Krull "yesterday" and today (above)

L et your biography rest on your desk or on a shelf for several weeks. Then, when you read it through, you will have fresh eyes to spot any flaws.

Edit your work

Reading your work aloud is one way to make the writing crisper. Now is the time to check spelling and punctuation. When the biography is as good as it can be, write it out again or type it up on the computer. This is your manuscript.

Think of a title

Great biography titles contain more than the subject's name. It is important to think of an intriguing, descriptive phrase to include in your biography's title. Think about titles you know and like.

Be professional

If you have a computer, you can type up your manuscript to give it a professional presentation. It should be printed on one side of white paper, with wide margins and double spacing. Pages should be numbered, and new chapters should start on a new page. Include your title as a header on the top of each page. At the front, have a title page with your name, address, telephone number, and e-mail address on it.

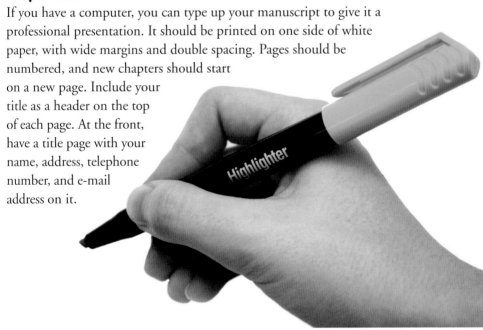

Make your own book

If your school has its own computer lab, why not use it to publish your biography? A computer will let you choose your own font (print style) or justify the text (making margins even, like a professionally printed page). When you have typed and saved the biography to a file, you can edit it quickly with the spelling and grammar checker, or move sections around using the cut-and-paste tool, which saves a lot of rewriting. A graphics program will let you design and print a cover for the book, too.

Having the biography on a computer file also means you can print a copy whenever you need one or revise the whole biography if you want to.

Tips and Techniques

Always make an electronic or printed copy of your biography before you give it to others to read. Otherwise, if they lose it, you may have lost all your valuable work.

REACH YOUR AUDIENCE

The next step is to find an audience for your biography. Family members or classmates may be receptive. Or you may want to share your work through a Web site, a literary magazine, or publishing house.

Some places to publish

There are several magazines and writing Web sites that accept biographical sketches from young authors. Some give writing advice and run regular competitions. Each site has its own rules about submitting work, so remember to read these carefully. Here are two more ideas:

- Send the opening chapter or concluding chapter to your school newspaper.
- Watch your local newspaper or magazines for writing competitions you could enter.

Finding a publisher

Study the market to find out which publishers publish biographies. Addresses of publishers and information about whether they accept submissions can be found in writers' handbooks in your local library. Keep in mind that manuscripts that haven't been asked for or paid for by a publisher—called unsolicited manuscripts—are rarely published. Secure any submission with a staple or paper clip, and always enclose a short letter (explaining what you have sent) and a stamped, self-addressed envelope for the biography's return.

omniscient viewpoint—an all-seeing narrator who sees all the characters and tells readers how they are acting and feeling

plot—the sequence of events that drive a story forward; the problems that the hero must resolve

point of view—the eyes through which a story is told

publisher—a person or company who pays for an author's manuscript to be printed as a book and who distributes and sells that book

simile—saying something is like something else, a word picture, such as "clouds like frayed lace"

synopsis—a short summary that describes what a story is about and introduces the main characters

third-person viewpoint—a viewpoint that describes the events of the story through a single character's eyes

unsolicited manuscripts—manuscripts that are sent to publishers without being requested; these submissions usually end up in the "slush pile," where they may wait a long time to be read

writer's block—when writers think they can no longer write or have used up all their ideas

Further information

Visit your local libraries and make friends with the librarians. They can direct you to useful sources of information, including magazines that publish biographies written by young people. You can learn your craft and read great stories at the same time.

Librarians will also know if any published authors are scheduled to speak in your area. Many authors visit schools and offer writing workshops. Ask your teacher to invite a favorite author to speak at your school.

On the Web

For more information on this topic, use FactHound.
1. Go to www.facthound.com
2. Type in this book ID: 075653366X
3. Click on the *Fetch It* button.
FactHound will find the best Web sites for you.

Read all the Write Your Own books

Write Your Own Adventure Story
Write Your Own Biography
Write Your Own Fairy Tale
Write Your Own Fantasy Story
Write Your Own Historical Fiction Story
Write Your Own Mystery Story
Write Your Own Myth
Write Your Own Realistic Fiction Story
Write Your Own Science Fiction Story
Write Your Own Tall Tale

Read more biographies

Aronson, Marc. *Up Close: Robert F. Kennedy.* New York: Viking, 2007.
Blumberg, Rhoda. *Shipwrecked! The True Adventures of a Japanese Boy.* New York: HarperCollins, 2001.
Byrd, Robert. *Leonardo: Beautiful Dreamer.* New York: Dutton Children's Books, 2003.
Cummins, Julie. *Tomboy of the Air: Daredevil Pilot Blanche Stuart Scott.* New York: HarperCollins, 2001.
Englar, Mary. *Benazir Bhutto: Pakistani Prime Minister and Activist.* Minneapolis: Compass Point Books, 2007.

Garrett, Leslie. *Helen Keller: A Photographic Story of a Life.* New York: DK Publishing, 2004.
Govenar, Alan. *Osceola: Memories of a Sharecropper's Daughter.* New York: Hyperion Books for Children, 2000.
Haugen, Brenda. *Geronimo: Apache Warrior.* Minneapolis: Compass Point Books, 2006.
Haugen, Brenda. *Henry B. Gonzalez: Congressman of the People.* Minneapolis: Compass Point Books, 2006.
Humphrey, Sandra McLeod. *Dare to Dream! 25 Extraordinary Lives.* Amherst, N.Y.: Prometheus Books, 2005.
Lalicki, Tom. *Spellbinder: The Life of Harry Houdini.* New York: Holiday House, 2000.
Lawlor, Laurie. *Shadow Catcher: The Life and Work of Edward S. Curtis.* Lincoln: University of Nebraska Press, 2005.
Márquez, Herón. *Roberto Clemente: Baseball's Humanitarian Hero.* Minneapolis: Carolrhoda Books, 2005.
McKissack, Patricia, and Frederick McKissack. *Red-Tail Angels: The Story of the Tuskegee Airmen of World War II.* New York: Walker and Company, 1995.
Myers, Walter Dean. *At Her Majesty's Request: An African Princess in Victorian England.* New York: Scholastic Press, 1999.
Rosinsky, Natalie M. *Amy Tan: Author and Storyteller.* Minneapolis: Compass Point Books, 2006.
Rosinsky, Natalie M. *Sarah Winnemucca: Scout, Activist, and Teacher.* Minneapolis: Compass Point Books, 2006.
Ryan, Pam Munoz. *When Marian Sang.* New York: Scholastic Press, 2002.
St. George, Judith. *Make Your Mark, Franklin Roosevelt!* New York: Philomel Books, 2007.
Weatherly, Myra. *Elizabeth I: Queen of Tudor England.* Minneapolis: Compass Point Books, 2006.

Books cited

Bolden, Tonya. *Maritcha: A Nineteenth-Century American Girl.* New York: Harry N. Abrams, 2005.

Freedman, Russell. *Confucius: The Golden Rule.* New York: Arthur A. Levine Books, 2002.

Freedman, Russell. *The Life and Death of Crazy Horse.* New York: Holiday House, 1996.

Freedman, Russell. *Lincoln: A Photobiography.* New York: Clarion Books, 1987.

Freedman, Russell. *The Voice That Challenged a Nation: Marion Anderson and the Struggle for Equal Rights.* New York: Clarion Books, 2004.

Freedman, Russell. *The Wright Brothers: How They Invented the Airplane.* New York: Holiday House, 1991.

Fritz, Jean. *Can't You Make Them Behave, King George?* New York: Coward, McCann & Geoghegan, 1977.

Giblin, James Cross. *Charles A. Lindbergh: A Human Hero.* New York: Clarion Books, 1997.

Giblin, James Cross. *Good Brother, Bad Brother: The Story of Edwin Booth and John Wilkes Booth.* New York: Clarion Books, 2005.

Giblin, James Cross. *The Life and Death of Adolf Hitler.* New York: Clarion Books, 2002.

Krull, Kathleen. *The Boy on Fairfield Street: How Ted Geisel Grew Up to Become Dr. Seuss.* New York: Random House, 2004.

Krull, Kathleen. *Lives of Extraordinary Women: Rulers, Rebels (and What the Neighbors Thought).* San Diego: Harcourt, 2000.

Krull, Kathleen. *Wilma Unlimited: How Wilma Rudolph Became the World's Fastest Woman.* San Diego: Harcourt Brace, 1996.

Nelson, Marilyn. *Carver: A Life in Poems.* Asheville, N.C.: Front Street Books, 2001.

Partridge, Elizabeth. *Restless Spirit: The Life and Work of Dorothea Lange.* New York: Viking, 1998.

Partridge, Elizabeth. *This Land Was Made for You and Me: The Life and Songs of Woody Guthrie.* New York: Viking, 2002.

Stanley, Diane. *Cleopatra.* New York: Morrow Junior Books, 1994.

Image credits

Steve Cukrov/Shutterstock, cover (top left); Library of Congress, cover (bottom and right, all), 5, 10–11, 13 (top), 17 (bottom), 18, 19 (top), 20, 22, 24 (top), 25 (top), 26–27, 28, 31, 32, 33, 34, 35, 37, 40, 43, 46, 61; Svetlana Zhurkin, 1, 23 (bottom), 38, 62; John Cross/The Free Press, 2; Aga & Miko Materne/Shutterstock, 4; Stephen Coburn/Shutterstock, 6 (top); Jason Stitt/Shutterstock, 6 (bottom); Thomas M. Perkins/Shutterstock, 7; Marc Romanelli/Photographer's Choice/Getty Images, 8 (top); Mark Kaufman/Time Life Pictures/Getty Images, 8–9; Pixelman/Shutterstock, 10 (left); Kristin Smith/Shutterstock, 11 (bottom); Mikhail Lavrenov/Shutterstock, 12; Line of Battle Enterprise, 13 (bottom); Sean Justice/Corbis/Royalty-Free, 14–15; Torsten Lorenz/Shutterstock, 16; Kenneth Graff/Shutterstock, 17 (top); Tamir Niv/Shutterstock, 19 (bottom); Lourens Smak/Alamy, 21 (top); Aaron Kohr/Shutterstock, 21 (bottom); DVIC/NARA, 23 (top); OlgaLis/Shutterstock, 24–25; Annenberg Rare Book and Manuscript Library, University of Pennsylvania, 29, 49 (top); Spela Marincic/Dreamstime, 30; Nick Alexander/Shutterstock, 36; Lordprice Collection/Alamy, 39; Jarvis Gray/Shutterstock, 42; Ian Shaw/Alamy, 44 (top), 57; Scott Rothstein/Shutterstock, 44 (bottom); Peter Baxter/Shutterstock, 45 (top); Terry Poche/Shutterstock, 45 (bottom); Suprijono Suharjoto/Shutterstock, 47, 51, 52 (top); Luis Francisco Cordero/Shutterstock, 48; GeoM/Shutterstock, 49 (bottom); Dóri O'Connell/Shutterstock, 50 (left); Jim Cummins/Taxi/Getty Images, 50–51; North Wind Picture Archives, 52 (bottom); Lorelyn Medina/Shutterstock, 53, 56 (top); Courtesy Houghton Mifflin Company, photo by Evans Chan, 54 (top); Courtesy Houghton Mifflin Company, photo by Alejandra Villa, 54 (bottom); Paul Brewer, 55 (top); Kenneth Krull, 55 (bottom); Johanna Goodyear/Shutterstock, 56 (bottom); Mario Lopes/Shutterstock, 58 (bottom); Jon Riley/Stone/Getty Images, 58–59; Michael Fuery/Shutterstock, 60; Kinetic Imagery/Shutterstock, 64.

Index